Contents

Welcome to the Rise and Shine Explorers Club

1 Trace and match.

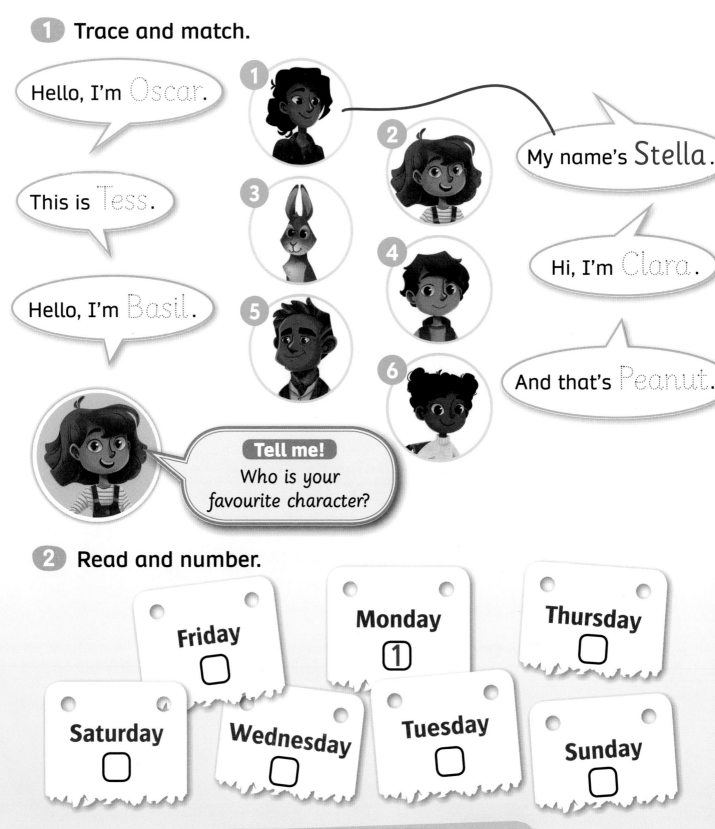

Hello, I'm Oscar.

This is Tess.

Hello, I'm Basil.

My name's Stella.

Hi, I'm Clara.

And that's Peanut.

Tell me!
Who is your favourite character?

2 Read and number.

Friday ☐

Monday ①

Thursday ☐

Saturday ☐

Wednesday ☐

Tuesday ☐

Sunday ☐

Extra time? Is it Monday today? Tell a friend.

3 Find and circle. Then trace and write the number.

eleven **11**

thirteen ☐

fifteen ☐

sixteen ☐

eighteen ☐

twenty ☐

Let's build!
This is my pen. It's red.

4  Listen and colour. Then say.

1    **2**    **3**   **4**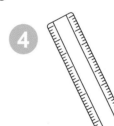

I can shine!

5 Trace, write and draw for you. Then say.

Hello! I'm

_____.

This is my

_____.

colour me

Say words that start with *p*.

Extra time?

Let's explore together

Lesson 1 ➡ Vocabulary

Let's review! PB p7 ➡ Find and trace.
Then say.

pen   ruler   rubber

1 Trace and number.

coat 1

scarf ☐

watch ☐

backpack ☐

trainers ☐

belt ☐

cap ☐

glasses ☐

Tell me!
What can you put
on your head? Circle.

glasses

cap

trainers

Extra time?
Say the words in alphabetical order.

1 **Listen and circle.**

1    **2**    **3**    **4**

Yes / No   Yes / No   Yes / No   Yes / No

2 **Trace. Then look and circle.**

Have you got …

1 trainers?
Yes, I have. / No, I haven't.

2 a scarf?
Yes, I have. / No, I haven't.

3 a belt?
Yes, I have. / No, I haven't.

4 a coat?
Yes, I have. / No, I haven't.

 **I can shine!**

3 🖊️ 💬 **Circle and colour.**
Then ask and answer.

Have you got a yellow belt?

Yes, I have.

 yellowbelt

 redscarf

 colour me

What are your favourite clothes? _____

Extra time?

5

1 PB p12–13 ➡ **Trace. Then read and circle.**

Have you got

glasses /
backpacks?

Have you got a

backpack /
mascot?

The Explorers Club has

got a mascot /
scarf!

2 ✏️ **Find and colour the caps. Then count and write.**

Let's imagine!
How many caps
have you got?

I can shine!

3 ✏️ 💬 **Draw three things.**
Then ask and answer.

Have you got
a scarf?

No, I haven't.

colour me

6

Which is your favourite story frame? Why? Tell a friend.

Extra time?

1 **Trace. Then look and write.**

short hair   **1**
long hair
dark hair
fair hair

2 **Follow, find and write. Then say.**

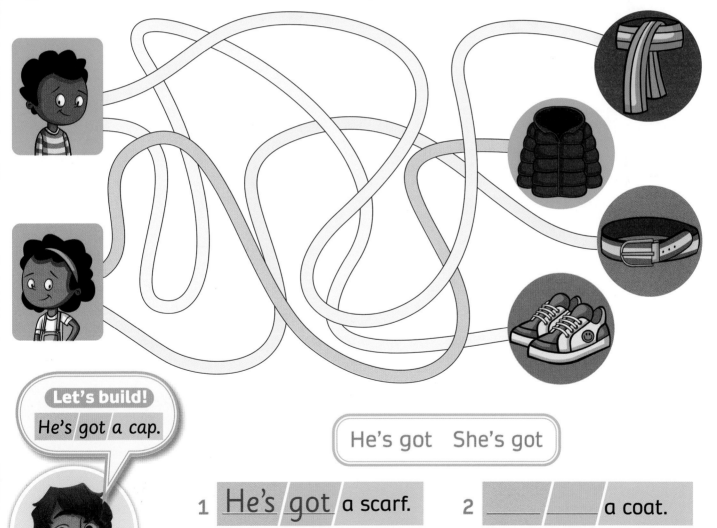

Let's build!

He's got a cap.

He's got   She's got

1 He's got a scarf.   2 _____ a coat.

3 _____ a belt.   4 _____ trainers.

Who's got long hair in your family? Tell a friend.

Extra time?

1 🎧 1.13 **Listen and match.**

1

2

My sounds

2 🎧 1.14 **Listen and repeat. Then circle.**

1  2  3  4 5

w / y   w / y   w / y   w / y   w / y

I can shine!

3 ✏ **Listen to a friend and draw. Then swap.**

He's got a long coat.

She's got a dark red scarf.

colour me

1 **Look and write. Then say.**

teacher   builder   ~~chef~~   explorer

1

2

3

4

He's a chef.

__chef__   _____   _____   _____

I can shine!

2 **Read and circle. Then act out.**

Think and share

What can you say about your friend's photo?

Look at this!

Oh, what a great photo! / This is for you!

colour me

When can you comment on a photo? Tell a friend.

Extra time?

1 Trace. Then tick (✓) or cross (✗) for you.

I've got ...

1 a backpack. ☐   2 trainers. ☐

3 glasses. ☐   4 a watch. ☐

5 a scarf. ☐   6 a coat. ☐

7 a belt. ☐   8 a cap. ☐

2 Look and write.

coat   dark   chef

1 She's a _____.

2 She's got a white _____.

3 She's got _____ hair.

3 Ask. Then tick (✓) or cross (✗) for your friend.

Have you got ...?

 ☐    ☐    ☐    ☐

He's got short, dark hair and a backpack. He's an _ _ _ _ _ _ _ _ _.

Extra time?

4 Stick and colour. Then play the game.

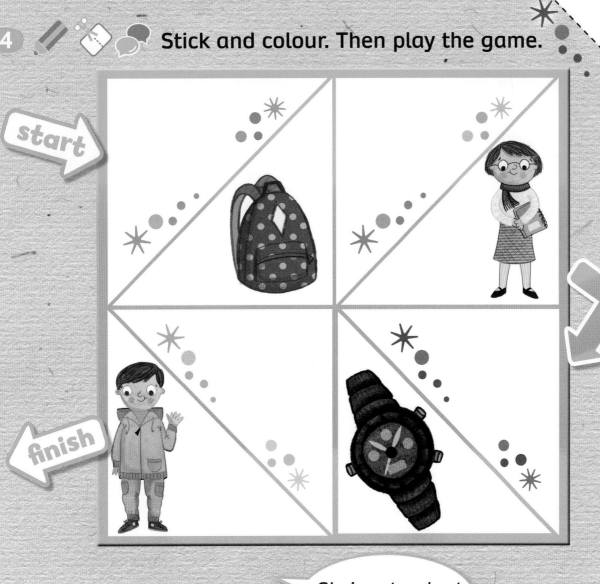

start

finish

> She's got a short green scarf.

> Different! She's got a short purple scarf.

5 Read. Then think and write.

My Things

I've got ...

_____
_____
_____
_____

I haven't got ...

_____
_____
_____
_____

Make a backpack. Then show and tell your family.

Home-school link

Let's be happy at home

Lesson 1 ➡ Vocabulary

Let's review! PB p10–11 ➡ Find and trace. Then say.

coat belt cap

1 Trace and number.

kitchen ☐   bedroom 1

living room ☐   bathroom ☐

garden ☐   hall ☐

garage ☐   stairs ☐

Tell me!
What can you find in a garden? Circle.

pyjamas

tree

flower

Extra time? Say the words in alphabetical order.

1 2.06 Listen and circle.

1
a 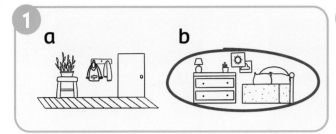 b

2
a 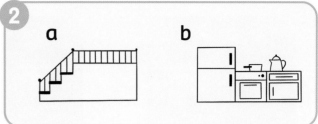 b

3
a 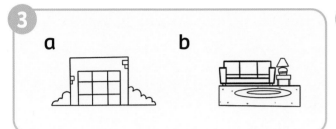 b

4
a 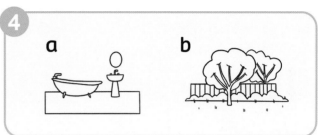 b

2 Circle and trace. Then look and write.

livingroombedroomgarden

1 Where's Mum? She's in the _____.

2 Where's Dad? He's in the _____.

3 Where's Grandma? She's in the _____.

I can shine!

3 Choose a room and write. Then ask and answer.

Where's Peanut?

He's in the _____.

colour me

Circle what's in your house: stairs / kitchen / garage. Tell a friend.

Extra time?

13

1 `PB p22–23` Trace. Then read and circle.

1

He's in the
bathroom /
kitchen.

2

Clara is in the
living room /
bedroom.

3

He's in the
garage /
garden.

2 Follow. Then circle.

Let's imagine!
Peanut is in the garden /
living room / kitchen.

I can shine!

3 Look at Activity 1. Write and say.

Peanut
_____ _____ _____
_____.

Oscar is in the
_____.

Tess is in
_____ _____
_____.

colour me

Which is your favourite story frame? Why? Tell a friend.

Extra
time?

1 Read and trace. Then number.

table 1   bed ☐   sofa ☐   lamp ☐

2 Read and circle. Then write.

Let's build!
Where's the book?
It's on the table.

on   next to

1 Where's the bed / table? It's _____ the sofa.

2 Where's the book / lamp? It's _____ the table.

3 Where's the watch / scarf? It's _____ the bed.

Where's your English book? Tell a friend.

Extra time?

1 **2.13** Listen and number.

My sounds

2 **2.14** Listen and repeat. Then circle.

1 r / l

2 r / l

3 r / l

I can shine!

3 ✏️ 💬 Draw two things. Write. Then ask and answer.

Where's the …?

It's _____
the _____.

colour me

1 **Match and write. Then say.**

| igloo | ~~treehouse~~ | cave | tent |

 1    2    3    4

<u>treehouse</u> _____ _____ _____

 a    b    c    d

> It's a treehouse.

I can shine!

Think and share
Do you like your home? Why?

2 **Read and write. Then act out.**

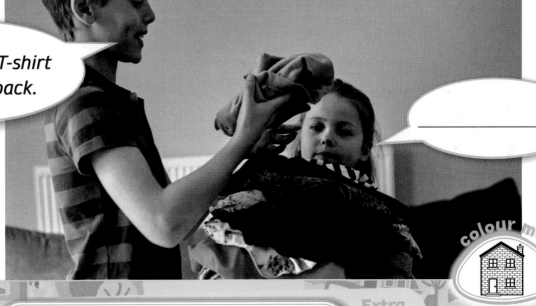

> Let's put the T-shirt in the backpack.

> _____

colour me

What rooms do you tidy at home? Tell a friend.

Extra time?

1 Find and circle. Then write.

a	b	a	t	h	r	o	o	m	c
l	i	v	i	n	g	r	o	o	m
r	o	p	s	t	a	i	r	s	t
e	g	a	r	d	e	n	w	y	r
o	o	m	g	a	r	a	g	e	d
c	y	h	a	l	l	o	n	y	s
d	f	g	b	e	d	r	o	o	m
i	k	i	t	c	h	e	n	l	g

1 bathroom   **2** _____

3 _____   **4** _____

5 _____   **6** _____

7 _____   **8** _____

2 🖊 💬 Draw and tick (✓). Then ask and answer.

Where's the …?	🎒	🖊
on the table		
on the bed		
next to the bed		
next to the lamp		

Where's the …?

It's …

18

It isn't a room. You can go up and down. They're _ _ _ _ _ _ _.

Extra time?

3 Stick and colour. Then play the game.

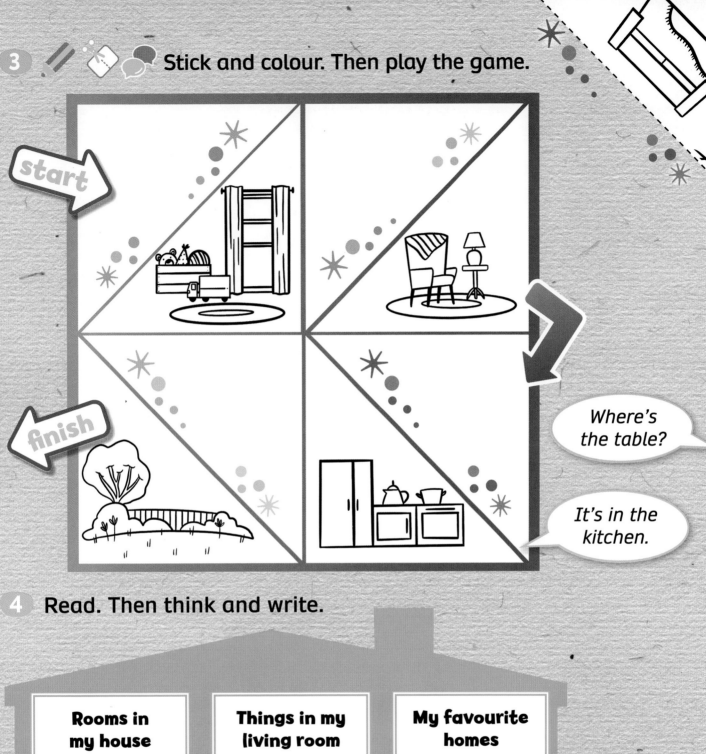

start

finish

Where's the table?

It's in the kitchen.

4 Read. Then think and write.

Rooms in my house	Things in my living room	My favourite homes
_____	_____	_____
_____	_____	_____
_____	_____	_____
_____	_____	_____

Make a tent. Then show and tell your family.

Home-school link

Review 1 Important to me

1 Read and trace. Then write the letter.

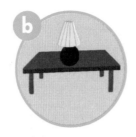

1 Have you got a backpack? Yes, I have.   [d]

2 Where's mum? She's in the bedroom.   [ ]

3 He's got dark glasses.   [ ]

4 Where's the lamp? It's on the table.   [ ]

5 Have you got white trainers? Yes, I have.   [ ]

6 Where's dad? He's in the garden.   [ ]

7 She's got a long scarf.   [ ]

8 The sofa is next to the table.   [ ]

2 (2.19) Listen and number. Then say.

   [ ]
   [1]
   [ ]
   [ ]

3 **Find and circle six words. Then write.**

HavehaslongoninWhere

1 <u>Have</u> you got a watch? No, I haven't.

2 She's got a _____ coat.

3 _____'s Mum?

4 Dad is _____ the kitchen.

5 My brother _____ got dark hair.

6 The lamp is _____ the table.

Mini-project

4 Draw your friend. Then write and say.

He's / She's got _____ _____.

What a _____ photo!

Time to shine!

5 Read, write and colour.

My things and My home

I can read ___ new words.

I can write ___ new words.

I can ask and answer questions about what I've got and where things are.

I can sing two new songs.

3 Let's explore nature

Let's review! PB p20–21 ➡ Find and trace. Then say.

bathroom   garden   garage

1 Look and write.

goose   chicken   turkey   goat   sheep   donkey   ~~cow~~   horse

1 COW

2 _____

3 _____

4 _____

5 _____

6 _____

7 _____

8 _____

chicken

Tell me!
Circle the odd one out.

donkey

horse

22

Say the words in alphabetical order.

Extra Time?

1  Listen and tick (✓) or cross (✗).

1  2  3  4  5  6

[✓] [ ] [ ] [ ] [ ] [ ]

2 ✏ What's on the farm? Trace, colour and write.

There's   There isn't

1 There's _____ a cow.   2 _____ a donkey.

3 _____ a sheep.   4 _____ a goat.

I can shine!

3 Look at Activity 2 and circle *Yes* or *No*. Then say.

There's a ...

There isn't a ...

1 There's a white goat.   Yes / No
2 There's a brown horse.   Yes / No
3 There's a brown cow.   Yes / No

colour me

Write your favourite farm animal. _____

Extra Time?

23

1 PB p34–35 **Look and read. Then write.**

sheep   cow   horse

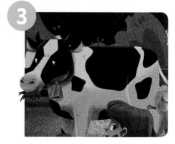

This is for the

_____.

Where's the

_____?

I can hear a

_____.

2 **Look and write.**

goat   horse   chicken

Let's imagine!
What food do they like?

1 This is for the _____.

2 This is for the _____.

3 This is for the _____.

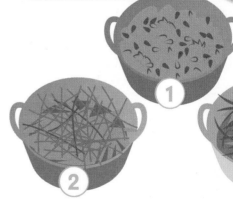

I can shine!

3 **Which animals are on the farm? Write and say.**

There's a _____,
a _____ and a
_____ on the farm.

24

Which is your favourite story frame? Why? Tell a friend.

Extra time?

1 **Look and write.**

bush   rock   ~~fence~~   wall

1 a <u>fence</u>

2 a _____

3 a _____

4 a _____

2 **Follow, find and write. Then say.**

Let's build!

There's a horse behind the wall.

1 There's a ___goose___ behind the ___rock___.

2 There's a _____ behind the _____.

3 Where's the _____? It's behind the _____.

4 Where's the _____? It's behind the _____.

Who is behind you now? Tell a friend.

Extra Time?

25

1 🎧 3.13 Listen and tick (✓) or cross (✗). Then match.

2 🎧 3.14 Listen and repeat. Then circle.

1   oo / ee

2   oo / ee

3   oo / ee

I can shine!

3 ✏️ Write. Then choose, circle and draw.

's   isn't

There _____ a cow.

There _____ a horse.

It's behind the
wall / fence / bush / rock.

colour me

1 Look, read and circle. Then say.

1

hear / (smell)

2

taste / see

3

hear / smell

4

taste / hear

5

taste / touch

> *I can smell a flower.*

Think and share
Close your eyes.
What can you hear?

I can shine!

2 Read, circle and write. Then act out.

> *Excuse _____.*
> *_____*
> *the park?*

> *It's behind the café.*

colour me

Where's your favourite park? Tell a friend.

Extra Time?

27

1 Look and write.

Across ➡	Down ⬇
2 	1
5	3
6	4
7	
8	

Crossword:
1 g o o s e (down)

2 Look and read. Then circle.

1 There's a bush.   ✓ / ✗

2 There isn't a wall.   ✓ / ✗

3 There's a donkey.   ✓ / ✗

4 There's a goose
  behind a fence.   ✓ / ✗

3 Look at Activity 2. Play *True* or *False* with a friend.

There's a goose.

True!

It's behind a bush.

False!

It's got 2 legs. It gives us eggs. What can you hear?

Extra
Time?

4 Stick and colour. Then play the game.

start

finish

There's a grey donkey.

Same!

It's behind the fence.

Different! It's behind the rock.

5 Read. Then think and write.

Animals

4 legs	2 legs

Make a farm animal mask. Then show and tell your family.

Let's try new activities

Let's review! PB p32–33 ➡ Find and write. Then say.

_____ _____ _____

1 **Look and write.**

| kick | swim | catch | skate | ~~skip~~ | climb | ride | swing |

1 <u>skip</u>

2 _____

3 _____

4 _____

5 _____

6 _____

7 _____

8 _____

Tell me! Think and write.

I do this with my _____

I do this with my _____

Say the words in alphabetical order.

Extra time?

1 **Listen and circle.**

1
a  b

2
a  b

3
a b

2 **Write. Then follow and circle.**

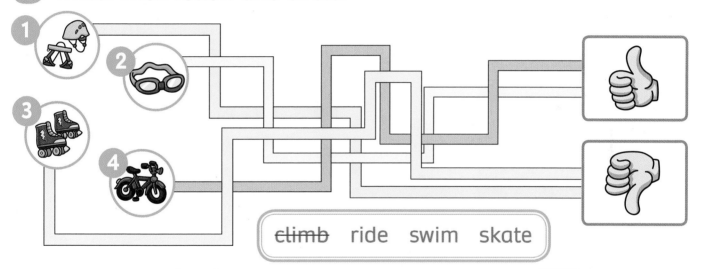

climb ~~climb~~ ride swim skate

1 Can you __climb__ ? Yes, I can. / (No, I can't)
2 Can you _____ ? Yes, I can. / No, I can't.
3 Can you _____ ? Yes, I can. / No, I can't.
4 _____ _____ a bike? Yes, I can. / No, I can't.

I can shine!

Can you swing?

No, I can't. But I can skate!

3 💬 **Guess the words. Then ask and answer.**

sgwni   blcim   estak

colour me

What can you do? _____

Extra time?

(31)

1 PB 44–45 **Look and read. Then write.**

swing   climb   swim

Can you

_____, Tess?

Can you

_____, Clara?

I can

_____.

2 **Look and write.**

climb   skate   swing

Let's imagine!

Which is the
odd one out?

_____   _____   _____

I can shine!

3 **Think and write. Then mime and guess with a friend.**

Can you
_____?

Can you
_____?

No, I can't.

Yes, I can.

colour me

Which is your favourite story frame? Why? Tell a friend.

**Extra
time?**

1 Look and write. **2** Number. Then circle and write.

| ~~tennis~~ a board game the guitar football |

play _____ **2**

play tennis **1**

play _____ **3**

Let's build!
Can he play football?
Yes, he can.

play _____ **4**

3 Can he / (she) play the guitar? — No, she can't. —

Can he / she play football? — _____

Can he / she play a board game? — _____

Can he / she play tennis? — _____

What can you play? Tell a friend.

Extra time?

1 🎧 4.13 Listen and tick (✓) or cross (✗).

	Ann	Bill
ride a bike	✗	
play football		
climb		
swim		

My sounds

2 🎧 4.14 Listen and repeat. Then match.

/ei/   /ai/

play   **climb**   **bike**   **day**

I can shine!

3 💬 Think and write. Then ask and answer.

This is Supergirl.

Can she skip?

No, she can't but she can play tennis!

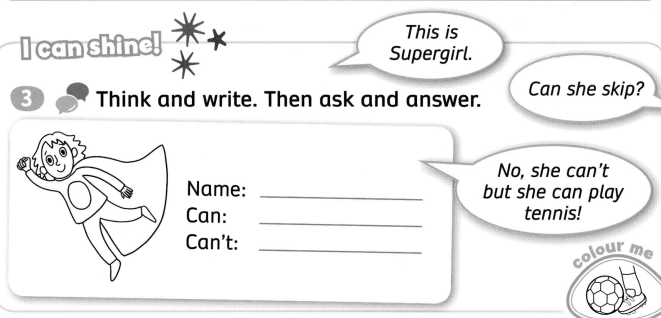

Name: _____
Can: _____
Can't: _____

colour me

1 **Write and number. Then say.**

> I can play the recorder.

| violin | drums | ~~recorder~~ | piano |

 a  b  c **1**  d

1    **2**    **3**    **4**

recorder _____ _____ _____

I can shine!

Think and share
What can you play with one friend, lots of friends or no friends?

2 **Read, write and circle. Then act out.**

> Would you like to join my club?

> Yes, of course! I'd _____ to join your _____.

Name: _____
Come to my club!
You can _____ and _____!

Answer: Yes, of course. / No, thanks.

colour me

Which is your favourite club? Tell a friend.

Extra time?

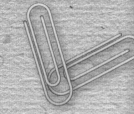

1 **Find and circle. Then write.**

v	n	s	s	v	h	l	s	y	f
m	e	w	p	j	f	k	w	u	j
c	l	i	m	b	l	i	i	j	v
e	z	n	n	u	r	c	m	m	c
k	w	g	a	n	s	k	a	t	e
r	i	d	e	a	b	i	k	e	n
j	j	c	a	t	c	h	k	b	k
w	c	s	k	i	p	e	u	z	i

1 climb

2 _____

3 _____

4 _____

5 _____

6 _____

7 _____

8 _____

2 **Look and tick (✓) or cross (✗) for you. Then say.**

> *I can kick. But I can't skip!*

3 💬 **Ask and answer. Then circle and write.**

> *Can you play the guitar?*

Friend's name: _____	
He / She can play _____	the guitar.
He / She _____	football.
He / She _____	a board game.

> *Yes, I can.*

36

You play it with your mouth. You can hear it. What is it?

Extra Time?

4 Stick and colour. Then play the game.

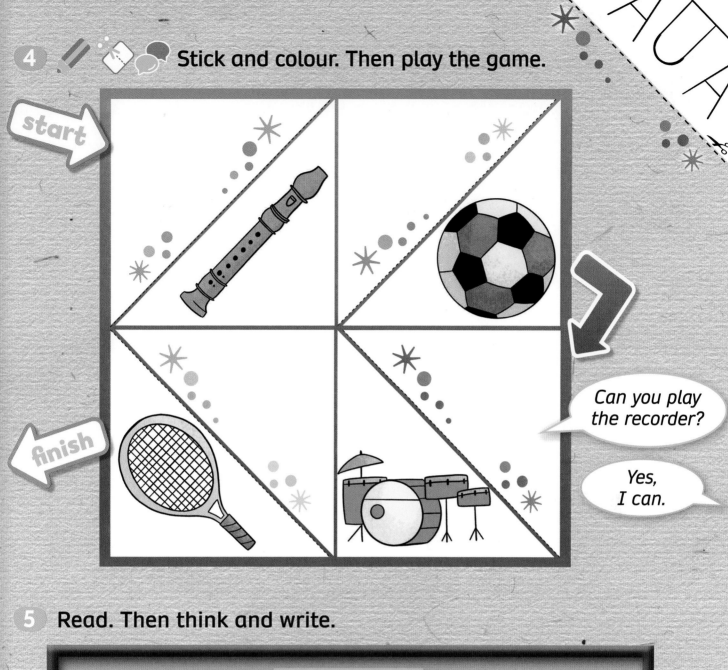

5 Read. Then think and write.

Make a board game. Then show and tell your family.

Home-school link

37

Review 2 — All about me

1 Read and write.

1 Can you _skate_? No, I can't.

2 There isn't a sheep. There's a _____.

3 She can't skip. But she can _____!

4 Can he _____ the guitar? No, he can't.

5 Look! There's a _____!

6 Look! There's a _____!

7 Can you _____? Yes, I can.

8 Where's the _____? It's behind the _____.

2 Listen and number. Then ask and answer.

Where's the farm?

It's behind the house.

3 Guess the words. Then write.

1 Listen! I can _hear_ a cow!

2 Can you _____ a bike?

3 Can he _____ the drums?

4 Look! I can _____ a chicken.

ehra

deri

ylap

ese

Mini-project

4  Draw and write. Then ask and answer.

Join the Explorers Club!

You can _____ and _____.

Would you like to join the Explorers Club?

Yes, of course! I'd like to join your club.

Time to shine!

5 Read, write and colour.

Farm animals and Actions

I can read ____ new words.

I can write ____ new words.

I can sing two new songs.

I can ask and answer questions about what there is and things I can do.

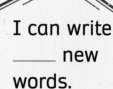

5 Let's share our food

Let's review! PB p42–43 ➡ Find and write. Then say.

_____ _____ _____

1 Look and write.

| orange | burger | fish | juice | ~~egg~~ | biscuit | cereal | carrot |

1 _egg_

2 _____

3 _____

4 _____

5 _____

6 _____

7 _____

8 _____

Tell me!

Circle the odd one out.

burger   orange

juice   fish

Say the words in alphabetical order.

Extra time?

1 **Listen and number.**

 ☐    ☐   1

2 **Read, write and circle.**

1 I'm eating / drinking _____ .   euijc

2 I'm eating / drinking a _____ .   rubreg

3 I'm eating / drinking _____ .   hisf

I can shine!

3 💬 **Choose and colour. Write for you. Then ask and answer.**

What are you doing?

I'm drinking _____ juice.

colour me

Write your favourite food. _____ Then say *I'm eating …*

1 `PB p56–57` **Look and read. Then write and number.**

washing   growing   eating

 **a**

 **b**

 **c**

Are you _____

my salad, Oscar?

I'm _____

my vegetables!

Are you _____

salad leaves, Oscar?

2 **Find two words. Then write.**

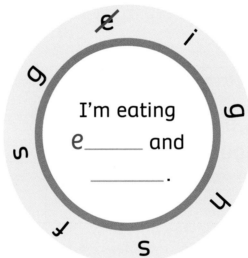

I'm eating

e_____ and

_____.

Let's imagine!
What are
you eating?

I can shine!

3 **Mime. Then ask and answer.**

What are
you doing?

I'm eating
cereal.

colour me

Which is your favourite story frame? Why? Tell a friend.

**Extra
time?**

1 **Look and write.** grow make ~~wash~~ cook

wash _____ _____ _____

2 **Look. Then read and write.**

Nora

Dad

Eva

Remi

Let's build!

Are you growing tomatoes?

Yes, I am. No, I'm not.

1 Are you growing strawberries, Nora? _Yes, I am._

2 Are you making biscuits, Eva? _____

3 Are you cooking fish, Dad? _____

4 Are you washing an apple, Remi? _____

Mime an action with a friend. Ask and answer _Are you ...?_

Extra time?

43

1 **(5.13)** Listen and circle.

1 a 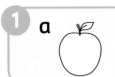 b

2 a  b

3 a   b

4 a   b

My sounds

2 **(5.14)** Listen and repeat. Then write *i* or *o*.

1 o

2

3

4

5

6

I can shine!

3 Choose. Then ask and answer.

Are you making a sandwich?

No, I'm not.

Are you eating an orange?

Yes, I am.

colour me

1 **Look and write. Then say.**

fruit vegetables
butter ~~flour~~

1

_____ flour _____

2

> I need flour.

_____

3

_____

4

_____

I can shine!

Think and share

What colour are your favourite foods? Do you like green vegetables?

2 **Read and write. Then act out.**

> I _____ fruit for the cake.

> OK, let's go _____!

colour me

Where do you go shopping? When? Tell a friend.

Extra time?

45

1 Look and write.

Across ➡ Down ⬇

2    1

3   2

5   4

6   7

```
          ¹f
      2 □ □ □ □ □ i
              s
   3 □ □ □  4 □ □ h
 5 □ □ □ □
              □
          6 □ □  7 □ □ □
              □
              □
```

2 Look and write. Then circle.

1 Are you _____ strawberries?
Yes, I am. / No, I'm not.   ✓

2 Are you _____ carrots?
Yes, I am. / No, I'm not.   ✗

3 Are you _____ a burger?
Yes, I am. / No, I'm not.   ✓

3 💬 Choose. Then ask and answer.

Orange!   *No, I'm not.*   *Yes, I am.*

Are you growing an orange?   *Are you eating an orange?*

It isn't a fruit. It's an orange vegetable. What is it?

Extra time?

4 Stick and put a tick (✓) or cross (✗). Then ask and answer.

Are you eating a carrot?

Yes, I am.

Are you drinking juice?

No, I'm not.

5 Read. Then think and write.

FOOD AND DRINK

At home	At parties	On holiday
_____	_____	_____
_____	_____	_____
_____	_____	_____

Make a paper salad. Then show and tell your family.

Home-school link

6 Let's have holiday fun

Let's review! PB p54–55 ➡ Find and write. Then say.

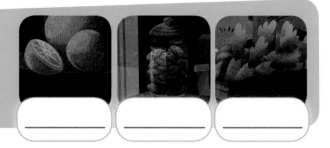

_____ _____ _____

1 Look and write.

| sleep   ~~holiday~~   beach   comics   sandcastle   shells |

1 go on <u>holiday</u>

2 build a _____

3 read _____

4 _____

5 collect _____

6 play on the _____

Tell me!

Write *a* for actions and *t* for things.

read [a]   shells [ ]

comics [ ]   collect [ ]

Extra time? Say the words in alphabetical order.

1 **Listen and tick (✓).**

1 a 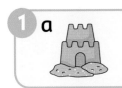 ☐ b 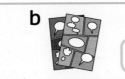 ✓

2 a  ☐ b  ☐

3 a  ☐ b  ☐

4 a 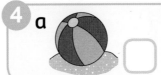 ☐ b  ☐

2 **Follow and find. Then circle.**

1 *I want to read comics / collect shells.*

2 *I want to read comics / collect shells.*

 **I can shine!**

3 **Look and write.**   **My holiday diary!**

I want to _____ on Monday.

_____ play on the beach on Tuesday.

_____ on Wednesday.   colour me

Do you collect things? What? Tell a friend.

Extra time?

(49)

1 `PB p66–67` **Look and read. Then write and number.**

to   shells   want   ~~sandcastle~~   football

I want to build a <u>sandcastle</u>*!*

I _____ to collect _____!

I want _____ play _____!

2 **Read and write for you.**

Let's imagine!
What do you want to do on holiday?

I want to

_____

_____.

I can shine!

3 Tick (✓) for you. Then say.

I want to read comics.

  □

 □

 □

 □

colour me

Which is your favourite story frame? Why? Tell a friend.

Extra time?

1 **Look and write.**

night   afternoon   evening   ~~morning~~

__morning__   _____   _____   _____

2 **Number to make sentences. Match. Then answer for you.**

a    ☐

b    **1**

c    ☐

1 play tennis   **2**
   in the morning?   **3**
   Do you want to   **1**

   __Yes, I do.__

3 in the evening?   ☐
   play the guitar   ☐
   Do you want to   ☐

   _____

2 read comics   ☐
   Do you want to   ☐
   in the afternoon?   ☐

   _____

Let's build!
Do you want to sleep in the afternoon?

Do you want to sleep in the morning? Tell a friend.

Extra time?

1   Listen and tick (✓) or cross (✗). Then ask and answer.

	morning	afternoon
⚽		
🎲		
🥽		

Do you want to play football in the morning?

Yes, I do.

My sounds

2   Listen and repeat. Then write *e* or *u*.

1 w e t   2 s__n   3 r__n   4 b__d

5 t__ddy   6 f__n   7 m__m   8 r__d

I can shine!

3 Choose and write. Then ask and answer.

Do you want to sleep at night?

Yes, I do.

_____ _____ _____ _____

(play)   (eat)   (climb)

(sleep)   (read)   (draw)

colour me

52

What do you want to do in the evening? Tell a friend.

Extra time?

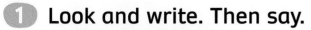

1 **Look and write. Then say.**

I like the sea. It's safe.

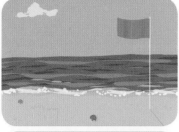

flag   safe   ~~sea~~   dangerous

1 Look at the _sea_____.
  It's _____.

2 Look at the red _____.
  The sea is _____.

I can shine!

Think and share
What things can you do on holiday that you can't do at home?

2 **Read and write for you. Then act out.**

Dear Max,
I like my holiday! I like the food and my new friends.
I don't like the hot weather.
Look at the photo. I'm swimming in the sea. It's great!
See you soon, Zoe

Dear _____,
I like my holiday!
I like _____ and
_____.
I don't like _____.
Look at the photo.
I'm _____.
It's _____.
See you soon, _____

colour me

Do you speak English on holiday? What can you say?

Extra time?

1 **Look and write.**

sleep   play on the beach   go on holiday
build a sandcastle   collect shells   read comics

1 <u>collect shells</u>

2 _____

3 _____

4 _____

5 _____

6 _____

2 **Write and circle for you.**
Then ask and answer.

you   Do   want

1 Do you <u>want</u> to play football in the afternoon?

Yes, I do. / No, I don't.

2 Do _____ want to sleep in the morning?

Yes, I do. / No, I don't.

Do you want to play football in the afternoon?

3 ____ you want to eat ice cream in the evening?

Yes, I do. / No, I don't.

4 Do you _____ to read comics at night?

Yes, I do. / No, I don't.

Yes, I do.

You build this on the beach. It's yellow. What is it?

Extra Time?

3 🖊 ✏️ 💬 **Stick and colour. Then tell a friend.**

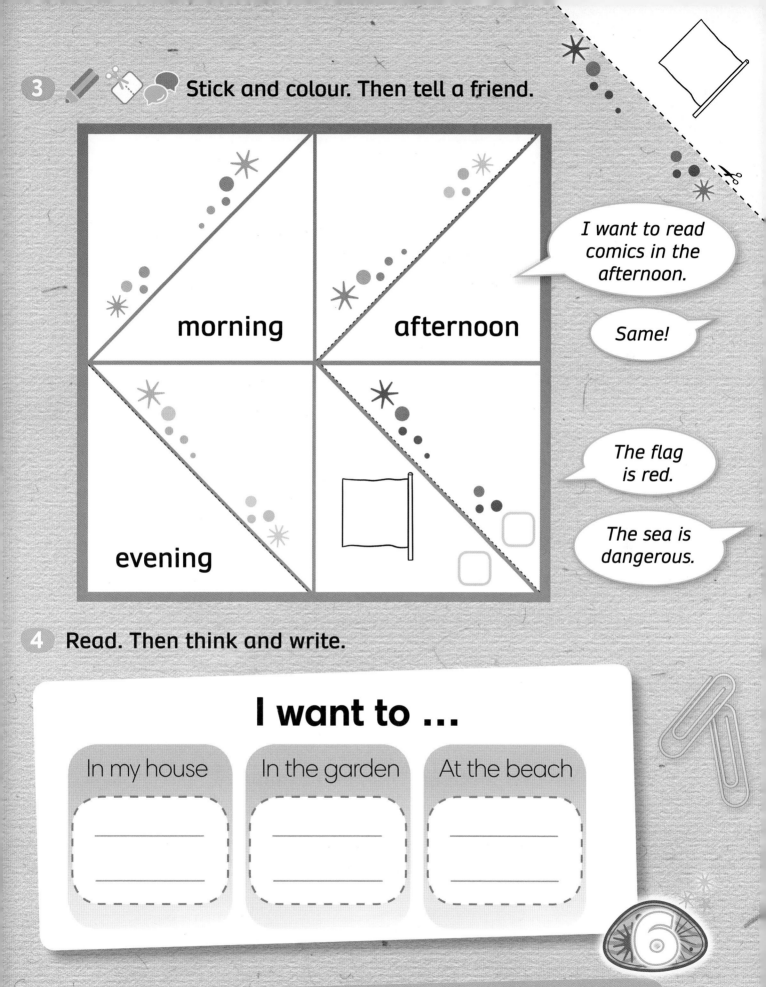

morning

afternoon

I want to read comics in the afternoon.

Same!

evening

The flag is red.

The sea is dangerous.

4 **Read. Then think and write.**

I want to ...

In my house	In the garden	At the beach
_____	_____	_____
_____	_____	_____

Make a holiday jigsaw. Then show and play with your family.

Home-school link

Review 3 — Around me

1 Look, read and write.

1 Are you drinking _____? Yes, I am.

2 I want to _____.

3 I'm eating a _____.

4 Do you want to _____ in the afternoon? Yes, I do.

5 I want to _____.

6 I'm _____.

7 I want to _____.

8 Are you eating? No, I'm not. I'm _____ eggs.

2 (6.19) Listen and number. Then point and say.

   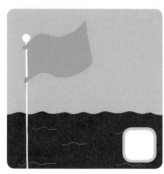

3 **Read and write.**

eating   holiday   ~~growing~~   beach

1 Are you <u>growing</u> tomatoes?

2 Do you want to play on the _____?

3 I'm _____ cereal.

4 I want to go on _____!

Mini-project

4  **Draw. Then write and circle.**

Happy holidays!

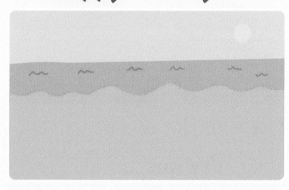

In the morning, I want to

_____.

In the afternoon, I want to

_____.

In the evening, I want to

_____.

I like / don't like my holiday!

Time to shine!

5  **Read, write and colour.**

Food and Holiday activities

I can write ____ new words.

I can read ____ new words.

I can talk about what I'm doing and what I want to do.

I can sing two new songs.

Goodbye from the Explorers Club

1 **Look and write.**

> cap   catch   ~~cook~~   build a sandcastle
> horse   living room   play the guitar   juice

1

cook

2

_____

3

_____

4

_____

5

_____

6

_____

7

_____

8

_____

2 **Think and write. Then say.**

I'm an explorer!

I want to ...	I've got ...
_____ _____	_____ _____
_____ _____	_____ _____

3 🎧 7.05 **Listen and tick (✓) or cross (✗).**

✗

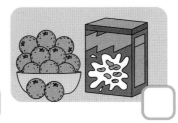

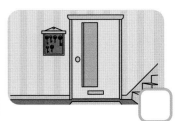

4 Number. Then circle.

This is for the donkey / fish.

Basil, do you want to play tennis / football?

My favourite room is the hall / kitchen.

Can you swim / swing, Clara?

Have you got a mascot / rabbit?

What are you growing / cooking?

Think and share

My favourite story is in Unit _____ .
My favourite character is _____ .

5   Listen and write. Then sing.

Happy   Peanut   explorer   see   Goodbye

_____, Stella, Tess and Clara,
Basil, Oscar and _____, too!
It's holiday time and I'm an _____!
Lots of things to _____ and do!
Goodbye! Goodbye! _____ holidays to you!

Let them shine!

1 **Look and write. Then listen and circle.**

| barbecue | balloon | ~~candle~~ | sparkler | cake | present |

1

candle

2

_____

3

_____

4

_____

5

_____

6

_____

*It's your birthday,
let's have fun!
A cake and a sparkler
for everyone!
Happy birthday,
happy birthday.
Happy birthday to you!*

Beautiful world

2 **Look and write. Then listen and circle.**

*This is a beautiful world!
How can it be?
Turtles in the ocean and
fish in the sea!
Animals on mountains
and hills and in trees!*

jungle	hill
mountain	ocean
desert	~~sky~~

1 sky   2 _____   3 _____

4 _____   5 _____   6 _____

Amazing oceans

3 🎧 *8.12* **Look and write. Then listen and circle.**

*I can see a (seahorse,)
an octopus, a dolphin
and a seal!
A shark and a whale –
at the bottom of the
deep blue sea!*

| dolphin ~~shark~~ |
| whale seal |
| octopus seahorse |

1 __shark__   2 _____   3 _____

4 _____   5 _____   6 _____

Let them fly!

4 🎧 *8.16* **Look and write. Then listen and circle.**

*I'm flying a kite,
I can see the (sun!)
I can see clouds in the sky!
It's day and I'm flying a kite.
Fly, kite, fly!
Fly, kite, fly!*

| stars moon |
| night sun |
| cloud ~~day~~ |

1 __day__   2 _____   3 _____

4 _____   5 _____   6 _____

Picture Dictionary

Welcome

Vocabulary

cloudy

rainy

pen

notebook

rubber

ruler

Unit 1

Vocabulary 1

backpack

belt

cap

coat

glasses

scarf

trainers

watch

Vocabulary 2

dark

fair

long

short

Unit 2

Vocabulary 1

bathroom

bedroom

garage

garden

hall

kitchen

living room

stairs

Vocabulary 2

bed

lamp

sofa

table

Unit 3

Vocabulary 1

 chicken
 cow
 donkey
 goat

 goose
 horse
 sheep
 turkey

Vocabulary 2

 bush fence

 rock wall

Unit 4

Vocabulary 1

 catch
 climb
 kick
 ride

 skate
 skip
 swim
 swing

Vocabulary 2

 board game
 football

 guitar
 tennis

Unit 5

Vocabulary 1

 biscuit
 burger
 carrot
 cereal

 egg
 fish
 juice
 orange

Vocabulary 2

 cook
 grow

 make
 wash

Unit 6

Vocabulary 1

 build a sandcastle

 collect shells

 go on holiday

 play on the beach

 read comics

 sleep

Vocabulary 2

 afternoon

 evening

 morning

 night

Celebration 1

Vocabulary 1

 balloon

 barbecue

 cake

 candle

 present

 sparkler

Celebration 2

Vocabulary 1

 desert

 hill

 jungle

 mountain

 ocean

 sky

Celebration 3

Vocabulary 1

 dolphin

 octopus

 seahorse

 seal

 shark

 whale

Celebration 4

Vocabulary 1

 cloud

 day

 moon

 night

 star

 sun